GREAT BEARDS OF HISTORY!

HISTORY

OLD BEARDS

ALSO HISTORY
PROF. BEARDY

FAMOUS PEOPLE WHO DIDN'T SHAVE

written and illustrated by Kellen Roggenbuck

ISBN: 978-1-0879-0895-3

DEDICATED TO LEVI,
THE ORIGINAL BEARD-GRABBER.

BLACKBEARD WAS A PIRATE WHO HAD A BLACK BEARD.

HE DIDN'T LIKE SHAVING OR EATING PICKLES.

No pickles, please and thank you!

ABRAHAM LINCOLN
HAD A BEARD
ON HIS CHIN
AND WAS
THE 16TH
PRESIDENT.

HE ALSO HAD
THE TALLEST
HAT OF
ALL THE
PRESIDENTS.

CHARLES DARWIN WAS
A SCIENTIST
WHO HAD
A BEARD.

HE STUDIED
BIRDS
AND
LOVED
PLAYING
BACKGAMMON.

FREDERICK DOUGLASS FOUGHT AGAINST SLAVERY AFTER ESCAPING BEING A SLAVE.

HE ALSO HAD A REALLY NICE BEARD.

THERE'S ALSO MY DAD.

HE CAN DO LAUNDRY WITHOUT EVEN SORTING THE COLORS.

WILLIAM SHAKESPEARE WROTE PLAYS AND POEMS.

Will, I am!

HIS BEARD WAS POINTY AND NO ONE EVER CALLED HIM BILL.

JOHANN STRAUSS
HAD A BEARD
EVERYWHERE
EXCEPT HIS
CHIN.

HE WROTE
CLASSICAL
MUSIC
AND
LOVED
POLKA.

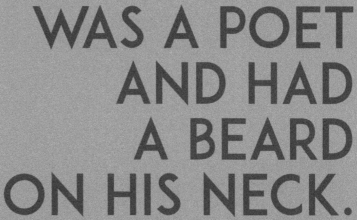

HENRY DAVID THOREAU WAS A POET AND HAD A BEARD ON HIS NECK.

HE ALSO HATED WEARING SOCKS.

DID I MENTION MY DAD?

HE CAN EAT A BURRITO WHILE HOLDING A BABY.

ANSEL ADAMS WAS A PHOTOGRAPHER WITH A SHORT BEARD WHO ONLY TOOK PICTURES IN BLACK AND WHITE!

ALEXANDER GRAHAM BELL
WAS THE INVENTOR OF
THE TELEPHONE.

HE HAD A
WHITE
BEARD
AND
WISHED
MORE
PEOPLE
WOULD
CALL HIM.

JOHN "GRIZZLY" ADAMS WAS A TRAINER OF GRIZZLY BEARS AND BEARDS.

HE ALSO ONCE LED A PARADE OF BEARS AND OTHER ANIMALS INTO SAN FRANCISCO.

OH, AND MY DAD KNOWS ALL THE WORDS TO THE REALLY OLD SONGS ON THE RADIO.

HARNAAM KAUR IS A BRITISH MODEL WITH A LOVELY BEARD.

SOMETIMES SHE EVEN WEARS FLOWERS IN IT.

BOB ROSS WAS A
PAINTER WHO HAD
A BEARD
AND A
TV SHOW.

HE WAS
ALSO A
FRIEND TO
MANY
SQUIRRELS.

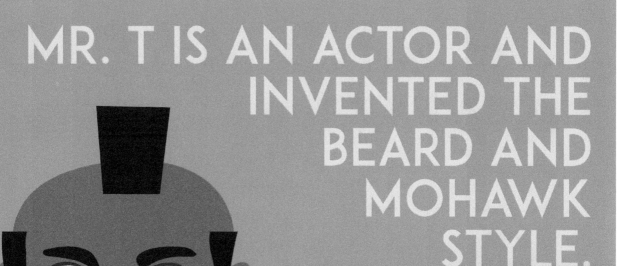

MR. T IS AN ACTOR AND INVENTED THE BEARD AND MOHAWK STYLE.

HIS NAME IS LAURENCE AND HE REALLY LOVES JEWELRY.

OH, AND MY DAD IS ALSO GOOD AT TELLING BEDTIME STORIES ABOUT ROBOTS.

DAD ALSO INVENTED THE CHILI BEAN AND NACHO CHEESE OMELETTE WE EAT FOR BREAKFAST WHEN MOM'S NOT HOME.

MY DAD AND HIS BEARD
MIGHT NOT
SEEM
FAMOUS
BECAUSE
HE DOESN'T
TRAIN BEARS
OR WEAR
A TALL
PRESIDENT
HAT,

THE END

BE SURE TO CHECK OUT OTHER BOOKS BY AUTHOR KELLEN ROGGENBUCK:

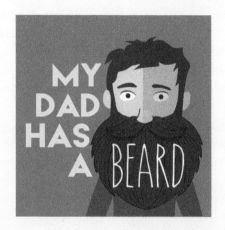

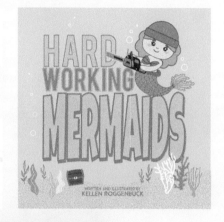

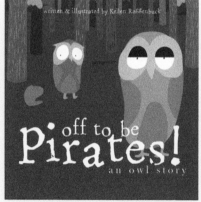

EACH BOOK IS WRITTEN TO BE FUN AND ENGAGING FOR READERS ADULT AND CHILDREN ALIKE, AND ARE AVAILABLE ON AMAZON!

CPSIA information can be obtained
at www.ICGtesting.com
Printed in the USA
LVHW070810160222
711184LV00009B/639